P9-CEV-319

WHAT'S COOKIN'?

Published by: A3TCO
PO Box 9181
Salem OR 97305
E-Mail: a3tco@teleport.com

Cover photography by Terry High

Printed in the United States - First Edition
Copyright 2001 by Teresa Trump

ISBN: 1-884366-04-X

Other books in the Uncle Bud series:

I Remember When
Lookin' Back
Sweet Memories
Reflections
Yesterdays

Hello there! Come on in and sit down. Most of the girls are here and some are coming from other areas close by.

Now, I hope you don't take offense at being called a girl, but some of us around the table here are 50 or older, and if we had a choice between being called "seniors" and "girls", well, we'll take the fairy tale.

This group of coffee cluckers gets together every now and again in my kitchen to talk about homemaking - or so we say. I guess in a way it's the womenfolk equal to Bud's early morning gossip sessions at the cafe. We like to give the boys some time to come up with new comebacks when the old duffers (that's them, including Bud) and the old duffettes (that us, including me) get together for coffee and a lively debate of words and wits.

A couple of years ago all the girls got together and pooled their holiday recipes in preparation for the baking season. Talking about those recipes brought back a lot of memories. So we decided we needed to have a recipe get together every few months or so. And now, passing on family cooking stories is an important part of what goes on around this table.

Today is recipe day and a chance to talk about your burnt offerings. What are those? Well, that's what every one of us offers to the cooking gods. Some of us stay in good standing by cremating, scorching, carmelizing, smoking, and torching up a food offering once a day, or week, in the kitchen. You're more than welcome to contribute -- we always have room for one more recipe and a good story.

Well, get your coffee poured and grab a seat. I see the recipes being laid on the table like poker chips.

CANNING AND FREEZING

Crock Pot Apple Butter

a crock full of apples
2 cups cider or apple juice
2 cups white sugar

1/2 cup brown sugar
2 tsp cinnamon
3/4 tsp cloves

Peel, core and chunk enough apples to fill a 4-6 quart crock pot to 1 inch of the rim. Add the cider, turn on low, put on the lid and cook for 12 hours. Stir in the rest of the ingredients and cook another 12-24 hours on low. Leave the lid open just enough for moisture to escape. Stir occasionally. When done, the butter should be thick and dark brown. Stir in any liquid left on top of the butter. Makes 4 pints. If you use a 4 quart pot, use 1 1/3 cups of cider and sugar. Reduce your spices.

Canning:

Store each batch of butter in the refrigerator until you have enough for a kettle full. Microwave your butter until its good and hot. Pour into hot sterilized half-pint or pint jars leaving 1/2 inch head space and process for 10 minutes in a boiling water bath.

...{{ Kyle's Relish }}...

When Kyle was about eight or nine, I recruited him to wash the cucumbers for pickling. Bud breathed a sigh of relief. He loved the finished product, but not all the hullabaloo to get there. Over the next few years, Kyle was the best helper a canning mom could have. However, somewhere along the way I had failed to notice it had quit being fun for him and was now a ... a ... a JOB! When folks want to get out of doing something, they work harder at getting out of it than if they just went ahead and finished the chore. And that's what Kyle did.

Since I had been playing nurse to my aunt and uncle and trying to help Bud out on the ranch, several chores had gone by the wayside, including the dirty clothes backed up on the washroom floor. After sorting the clothes, I asked Kyle to load the washer, put in the soap and turn it on. It didn't take Kyle long to figure out a plan. Over the next couple of washing days, he watched the agitator go through every cycle and had come to the scientific conclusion that this definitely was the way to go.

On a lovely, early summer morning, I had picked the cucumbers and placed the full lugs in the cellar to stay cool. My goal was to get them started soon or they would go hollow on me. Just as I finished making the brine, my aunt phoned for help with my uncle's medical needs, and I ran out the door, hollering back at my son to please wash and drain the cucumbers so I could get started the minute I got back.

There was no time like the present to put the theory to the test. He went down to the cellar and brought up a few lugs of cucumbers. After dumping them in the washer, he spun the dial for the gentle wash cycle. Kyle had left the lid up so he could watch his invention and make adjustments.

Well, they did real good until the spin cycle. When the spinner kicked in, cukes went flying and leapfrogging through the air. Our manx cat, Max, asleep in one of the laundry baskets at the time was confronted by a barrage of cucumber missles and tore out of the washroom, knocking over the mops and brushes and sending the rugs and cat food flying.

My son slammed the washer lid down and imprisoned what cucumbers were left. He managed to get the washer stopped but not before he had made relish.

Zucchini Relish

This is a good way to use the larger zucchini. Don't use the "club" sized squash with thickened skin. It's too tough. Wash the zucchini and drain. Split them down the middle and scrape out the inside seed section. Chop the zucchini into chunks for grinding. You can grind coarse or fine, whichever kind of relish you prefer.

10 cups zucchini ground   1 red pepper minced fine
4 cups onion ground

Add 5 tablespoons of salt to the mixture and let stand overnight in a cool place or the refrigerator. Drain off the salt water and add cold water and rinse the ground relish. Drain in a very fine sieve so as not to lose the pulp. Place the ground mixture in a stainless steel kettle and add:

2 1/2 cups vinegar	6 cups sugar
1 tsp celery seed	1 tsp turmeric
1 tsp nutmeg	3 tablespoons cornstarch
1-2 tsp fresh ground black pepper	

Place a heat grate over your burner to prevent relish from scorching. Cook on medium high until clear. Pour into pint or quart hot sterilized jars and seal. Process in a boiling water bath 15 minutes. Makes 8 pints.

Frozen Corn

2 tablespoons sugar	1 cup water
1/4 lb butter - real thing	1 1/2 tsp salt
8 heaping cups of fresh cut corn	

Combine ingredients in a stainless steel kettle. Boil for 5 minutes, stirring so it doesn't scorch. Quickly cool the kettle of corn in ice water. Package corn in freezer bags or boxes and freeze immediately.

Mom's Sweet Pickles

Fill a quart jar with small cucumbers that have been washed and rinsed several times. Add:

1 cup white vinegar	1/4 tsp powdered alum
1 tablespoon each pickling spices and noniodized salt	

Add enough water to fill the jar and seal tightly. Store in a cool dry place for 3 months. Pour out liquid and rinse out all the spices. Slice cucumbers back into the jar and add 1 cup of sugar. Let it stand for 24 hours. Shake occasionally to dissolve the sugar. Store in the refrigerator. As one jar is used, add the sweet liquid to the next jar and add sugar as needed.

Pickled Asparagus

2 cups asparagus washed and trimmed

1/2 cup boiling water	1/8 tsp pepper
2/3 tablespoon sugar	1/8 tsp dill
1/2 tsp salt	1/2 cup vinegar
1 clove garlic halved	
1 tsp pickling spice (optional)	

Combine the water, sugar, salt, pepper, dill and spices. Cook just until sugar dissolves, then add the vinegar. Set in refrigerator to chill. Blanch the asparagus 2 minutes and cool quickly. Pack into jars and add the garlic. Cover with cold pickling solution and keep in refrigerator. Add more garlic or dill for your tastebuds.

Canning: heat pickling solution and pour over the hot blanched asparagus leaving 1/2 inch head space, seal and process in boiling water bath for 10 minutes.

Apple Pie Filling

7 quarts - you will need 21-25 apples
About 3 large apples per jar

4 1/2 cups sugar	1 tsp salt

1 cup cornstarch   3 tablespoons lemon juice
2 tsp cinnamon   1/4 tsp nutmeg
2-3 drops yellow food coloring (if needed)
5-6 lbs of apples, peeled, cored and sliced

In a large saucepan blend the sugar, cornstarch, salt, spices. Stir in 10 cups of water. Cook and stir until thick and bubbly. Add lemon juice and food coloring. Pack the apples in hot sterilized jars leaving 1/2 inch head room. Pour hot syrup over the apples. Run a knife down in the jars to remove any bubbles and distribute syrup evenly. Process in a boiling water bath for 20 minutes.

You can also remove the syrup from the stove and add all the apples to it and then fill the jars. However, you may not get an even distribution of apples to syrup.

Suggested uses for filling:

Cake: Use in place of the applesauce. Cut the sugar in your cake recipe and delete your spices. Add to a chocolate cake mix for spicy flavor.

Cobbler: Grease a 9x12 pan and pour a quart in the pan. Cover with your favorite cobbler topping and bake as directed for your cobbler.

Dinner Crepes: Use as a filling with sour cream.

Meats: Heat the apple mixture for a condiment.

Pie: Just open a jar and pour in a pie shell. Bake at 400 for 50 minutes.

Shake: Blend with vanilla ice cream and milk.

Spiced applesauce: Put it through a blender.

Yogurt: Fold into yogurt for a snack.

BREADS and ROLLS

Everyone has a favorite cinnamon roll recipe, and so does Gladys. She's added it to our mix today but insists on telling the tale behind it.

...{{ Cinnamon Roll Shenanigans }}...

"Pete and I were living out in the wilds of nowhere. One of the big name farmers in the area had a wife who was known county-wide for her cinnamon rolls. I'll call her Nola, to protect the innocent. She brought her cinnamon rolls to every bake sale and cake auction whether it was church, high school, you name it. There was a clamoring among the men when they saw those mouth-watering, nut glazed rolls arrive. I swear the coffee output tripled at the high school concession stand when Nola's rolls were around.

"After one particular high-pitched auction at the school to help out the freshman class, I went up to her and asked her if I could have her roll recipe. She was flush with victory over the attention and the money her rolls had brought in. A neighborly exchange was not in the picture.

"Gripping my right arm with her left hand, nails sinking in like a tiger's claws, she smiled cattily and said, *My dear Gladys, this recipe has been in my family for years and I **don't** share it with anyone.* Purring softly, she continued, *You do understand, hmmm?*

"Well, the gauntlet had been thrown and I had my hackles up. I was a good cook and by golly that recipe was gonna be well known by the time I got through with it.

"Pete bought some of Nola's rolls for me everytime she trotted them out. He said we were going to the poorhouse and lamented he was taking a bite out of his leg for lunch because all his money went for rolls.

"I tested, tasted, froze and unfroze those rolls, matching ingredient for ingredient. It took me six months to get it right - a lot of flour, yeast and kneading. Then it was time for the ultimate test. I promised Pete if he would buy rolls one more time, it would be the last. He closed his eyes as if in prayer, and I heard him whisper, *Thank you, thank you.*

"While he was at the local auction where the church group was having the bake sale, I cooked up my own and put them in the back room to cool. That evening we had neighbors over and after supper, I glazed the rolls, sprinkled on the nuts and served them with coffee.

"Man, that Nola can make a roll, can't she?

"We heard she sold out early at the bake sale.

"Gladys, you must have been there pretty early to snatch these up.

"No, I had some things to do, I said, looking straight at my husband.

"Well... Pete had a puzzled look on his face. *I was there, but I didn't get to the baked goods right away. Got caught up in some lively local politics.* Shrugging his shoulders and an apology in his eyes, he said, *By*

9

the time I got there, the bake sale was pretty much over.

"Then how did you get a sample of Nola's rolls?

"Uhh, I didn't ... I didn't get any rolls. Pete looked at me and I could see the light bulb coming on.

"Well, if these aren't Nola's ...

"Pete was grinning and then he started laughing. *Well, from now on, when you come to our house, you can have all the cinnamon rolls you want. Gladys just broke Nola's secret recipe.* Wiping tears from his eyes, he sighed, *I'm glad that's over. I think Nola was beginning to think I was sweet on her. And after all that roll buying, she would not look fondly on a poor man.*

"And today I am doing my duty by adding this recipe to be spread far and wide. Enjoy, folks."

Best Ever Cinnamon Rolls

1 pkg active dry yeast	1/4 cup sugar
1/4 cup warm water	1 tsp salt
1 cup scalded milk	1 tsp vanilla

1/4 cup shortening or oil
2 eggs beaten
3/4 cup mashed potatoes (leftover or instant)
5 to 6 cups sifted bread flour

Toppings

1/3 cup melted butter	1/4 cup nuts fine chopped

1-2 cups bread crumbs with cinnamon

Dissolve the yeast in warm water. Let rise for 10 minutes. Combine the milk, vanilla, shortening, sugar and salt. Cool to lukewarm. Sir in yeast, potatoes and eggs. Gradually add enough flour to make a soft dough. Turn out on floured surface and knead until smooth and satiny (about 10 minutes). Place in lightly greased bowl. Turn over to grease top. Cover and let rise in warm place until double, about 1 to 1 1/2 hours. Turn out on lightly floured board and roll to 1/2 inch thick.

For Sweet Rolls: Cut into strips. Twist and shape into a round, starting at the center and working out. Dip into melted butter, then bread crumbs with cinnamon. Place on greased baking sheet. Let rise 30 minutes and bake in a preheated 350 degree oven for 20 minutes. Cool on a pastry rack. Drizzle with Glaze (see below) and sprinkle with fine chopped nuts.

For Raised Doughnuts: Cut with a 4 inch doughnut cutter. Let rise 30 minutes. Fry in hot fat 375 degrees and then drain on several thicknesses of paper towels. Drop the hot doughnuts into glaze and drain on a pastry rack. Makes 3 1/2 dozen.

GLAZE: Drizzle over sweet rolls hot from the oven or dip the doughnuts in it.

1 lb powdered sugar   6 tablespoons water
1 tablespoon vanilla

Hints: Use a pastry brush to brush on the butter or use butter spray. Sprinkle the crumbs by hand or use a shaker with big holes in the lid.

...{{ The First Loaf }}...

Our house is so fast paced these days, with the grandkids around, the boys running the ranch and Bud at the cafe. I wanted more quality time with them and finally broke down and bought a bread machine. But I have to tell one on myself before I hand over my favorite recipe.

When I smell bread baking it brings me back to the first time I decided to make bread for my mother. She was a single parent schoolteacher trying her best to raise me alone. Mother had been working long hours right at the end of the school year. The classrooms were going to be repainted and retiled so everything had to be packed and stored. On top of that, she was trying to finish student records and meet with all the parents about their kids and their school placement for the next year.

I knew that she had breadmaking in mind for the weekend, but there was one more parent conference scheduled for Saturday. A forest fire up in the hills west of town had been raging since the day before, and the temperature had stayed steady in the 100 degree range. However, this particular Saturday morning, the air had cooled a bit so I decided I would surprise her and make the bread that morning before it really was too hot in the house to bake.

Having helped her measure ingredients and knead bread countless times, it was going to be quick and easy. In my fantasy, I would bring her a slice of hot bread with some iced tea while she put her feet up and relaxed. The exact amounts to be used were a little fuzzy, so all the yeast in the big can was added just to make sure. Everything went together fine but the bread didn't raise. I waited and waited and nothing happened. Pondering over whether I should make another batch, I realized there was no more flour or yeast. Then it hit me - with the kitchen a mess and no ingredients to make more bread - I might be in big trouble. There was a flurry of dishwashing and kitchen cleaning. The empty flour sack was disposed of and the yeast can carefully placed back in the cupboard as though nothing had been disturbed.

But what to do with the bread that refused to rise? I stared out the kitchen window trying to figure out what to do next. I spotted the new clothesline my mother's friend had helped to set up and an idea started taking shape. I went outside and saw that the dirt under the clothesline was still loose and would be easy to dig up. I grabbed a spade from the storage shed and got to work. When the hole seemed deep enough, I dumped the big batch of stubborn unrisen dough into the hole and covered it up. Everything was returned to its rightful place and the world looked normal.

By the time mother arrived in the early afternoon, it was already 103 degrees and not a breath of air stirring. She had washed clothes early that morning and left them in the washer so they could be hung out on her return home. I was playing with paperdolls in the bedroom when she took the clothes out to the line. It was my misfortune that mother dropped a clothespin and while bending down to pick it up saw this mound of dirt rising up to meet her. In fact, the dirt was rolling off the top of the now rapidly rising bread dough. There was a scream and then "Martha Jane!" The jig was up.

The long explanation was punctuated by me crying and lots of hugs from her. No recriminations passed her lips. We made out a list together and then shopped at the nearby corner grocery. She supervised and I was the maker and baker of bread that day. Years later when we would talk about this over coffee, she said she realized that I had always taken part in the process but never from beginning to end. I had pieces of it, but not the whole picture. There is no failure, just varying degrees of success.

Combo Oatmeal Bread

1/3 cup sour cream	1 tsp salt
1 1/3 cups water	1 1/2 cups wheat flour
2 tablespoons oil	1 1/2 cups white flour
1 tablespoon sugar	1 pkg quick rise yeast
1 cup quick rolled oats	

Place the sour cream, water and oil in the bread pan first. Add sugar, salt, flour, oats and then the yeast. I use the basic rapid rise setting for a 1.5 lb loaf. You can use whole wheat rapid rise, but your loaf will be more dense. Bake according to your machine's directions. Great for sandwiches.

SOUPS AND CHOWDERS

ChickPea Soup

2 cups chicken jellied broth   1/2 cup water

1/2 tsp garlic powder   1/2 tsp onion powder
1 can blackeye peas w/ juice   1 can stewed tomatoes
1 pkg frozen rice and veggies

Bring to a boil in a kettle. Cover and simmer for 30 minutes. Salt to taste.

...{{ Zuchinni, anyone? }}...

We finally agreed this year that only two gardeners need to plant zuchinni for all of us who are still canning in this modern day of computers. Last year, Joe's mom came to visit about the time Marge was putting in her vegetable garden. Marge had only planted one hill of zuchinni, knowing that if it croaked, we would all be glad to share our harvest. Like all mothers, Joe's was never short on advice, and she decided to plant five hills - just in case.

Well, it was a good garden year for squash. Yeppers, Marge was overrun with the big Z. She was holding any kind of get together at her house she could think of - the grand door prize being zuchinni. In desperation, Marge set up a roadside stand in front of their house until Deputy Bill Larson said she needed a permit to sell "produce" or face a fine. No zuchinni was worth it.

In the meantime, Joe begin to wonder why none of their friends stopped by the store to chat anymore. When he went to the cafe, the men would back up, look him over, and ask if he was carrying anything. That went on until he happened to be home at the right time when a load of squash was hauled in from the garden. He told Marge the squash infestation was over! No more! He was beginning to feel like he was on parole every time he went to the cafe.

Marge worked this recipe over to get rid of some of the excess.

Almost Split Pea

3 cups young zucchini chopped
2 strips diced uncooked bacon
2 beef bouillon cubes
1 small onion chopped
1 clove garlic minced

2 cups water
2 tsp parsley
1/2 tsp basil
1/2 tsp season salt
1/4 tsp salt & pepper

Put all the ingredients in a large pot and cook until zucchini and onion are tender. While warm, pour the mixture into your blender and blend until smooth. Be sure your blender can "take the heat" of the soup. Pour into bowls and top with your choice of grated cheese or sour cream. Serve with garlic toast or a vegetable herb bread.

BREAKFAST

Bud's Coffee Cake

Preheat oven to 375 degrees
Grease 8 inch square or round cake pan

2 cups flour
1/2 cup sugar
1/2 tsp salt
2 tsp baking powder
1/2 cup milk*

2 eggs*
1/3 cup oil
1 tsp vanilla
1/2 tsp lemon extract
1 cup blueberries (optional)

*Substitute sour cream and water for the milk and use egg replacement or whites.

Sift the dry ingredients. Mix together the eggs, milk, oil and flavoring. Add to the flour mix and stir. Fold in the blueberries. Spread in the prepared pan. Sprinkle with topping. Bake 35-40 minutes. Serves 6-8.

Topping:

1/2 cup brown sugar	1/4 cup butter
1 tsp cinnamon	1/4 cup nuts chopped fine

Blend together. Nuts are optional.

Surprise Me Muffins

Preheat oven to 400 degrees
Grease muffin tins or use colored cupcake papers

1/2 cup lite sour cream	3 tsp baking powder
1/2 cup water	1/4 cup sugar
1 egg	1/2 tsp salt
2 cups sifted flour	1/4 cup soft margarine

Whisk sour cream, water and egg. Sift dry ingredients and cut in the margarine. Add egg mixture. Stir until moistened. Batter will be lumpy. Drop a tablespoonful in each muffin cup. Add a tablespoon of jam, jelly, or chopped nuts with brown sugar and cinnamon to the center of each muffin. Fill each 2/3 full with remaining batter. Bake 20-25 minutes. Makes 12 muffins.

Popovers

Preheat oven to 375 degrees
Heavily butter 6 muffin cups or custard cups

In a blender combine and blend until smooth:

3 eggs   1 cup flour unsifted
1 cup milk   1/4 tsp salt
1 tablespoon oil

Make herbal by adding 1 small clove of pressed garlic and rosemary or oregano leaves. Pour the batter into the cups. Bake about 60-70 minutes until puffed and brown. About 5 minutes before removing from oven, pierce with wooden skewer in several places. Serve hot with syrup, jam or fill with scrambled eggs, shrimp dip, meat or cheese.

DRESSINGS

Celery Seed Dressing

3/4 cup oil   1/3 cup white vinegar
1/2 cup sugar   2 tsp mustard
1 tsp celery seed   3/4 tsp salt
1/3 cup finely minced onion

Blend in your blender and serve immediately over tossed greens, tomato and onion rings, or toss with veggie mix, refrigerate and serve cold.

Thousand Island - on the skinny side

1 cup non fat sour cream   1 tsp mustard
1/3 cup relish   1/3 -1/2 cup catsup
1 tsp onion powder   1 tsp Worcestershire
1/4 tsp paprika   1/4 tsp garlic powder
1 heaping tablespoon real mayonnaise

Mix together. Salt, pepper and more spices to taste.

Flamin' French Dressing

1 regular can tomato soup	1/2 cup sugar
1/2 cup oil	1 tsp paprika
1 tsp salt	1 tsp garlic powder/salt
1 tablespoon Worcestershire	1/2 cup vinegar

Blend in your blender until smooth. Great on salads and vegetables. Keep refrigerated and shake well before using.

Low Fat Dressing Base

1 16 oz carton of nonfat or 2% cottage cheese
1/3 cup buttermilk

To this base add 1 tablespoon of any herb or cheese that strikes you as good. Blend smooth in blender. Salt and pepper to taste.

SAUCES AND GLAZES

Sweet Spicy Glaze

1/2 cup apple jelly	1/2 tsp garlic minced
2 tablespoons spicy mustard	1/4 tsp salt
1/4 cup finely chopped apple or applesauce	

Heat through and serve with meat and on veggies, too.

Sweet 'n Sour - from your cupboard

1/4 cup white vinegar	3 tablespoons catsup
1/4 cup apricot preserves	1/4 cup marmalade
1/8 tsp salt	

Mix together and use on meat, veggies or in stir fry dishes. Toss a couple of tablespoons with mixed melon and citrus fruits. Can make a whole gob or just enough for a couple of folks.

Barbeque Sauce - in a pinch

2 tablespoons Worcestershire   1 cup catsup
1/4 cup honey or brown sugar   3 drops liquid smoke
1/2 tsp mixed herb seasoning

Options: Pineapple bits, minced onion or garlic.

Mix together and add salt and pepper to taste. Use as a basting for meats, spice up veggies, slather on hot dogs, sausages, etc.

Tartar Sauce

3 tablespoons lite sour cream   2 tsp relish
1 tsp real mayonnaise   1/2 tsp mustard
1 tsp dill pickle juice or vinegar   1/2 tsp paprika
1 tsp finely minced onion
salt and pepper to taste

Mix and let set up for one hour. I can't say how long it lasts because there is never any left over! You can double or triple this as needed.

VEGETABLES

Classy Baked Cabbage

Preheat oven to 350degrees

1 large head cabbage   1/2 cup cracker crumbs
2 cups milk or broth   1 cup cheese

1 tablespoon butter   salt and pepper
1 tablespoon flour

Coarsely chop the cabbage and steam to wilt. Cook the butter, flour and milk until creamy smooth. Add the cabbage and stir until coated with the sauce. In a greased baking dish, place layers of cabbage, salt and pepper, crumbs and cheese. Spray with some butter spray and bake until brown. Serves 4-6.

BBQ Bud Spuds

Preheat oven to 375 degrees
Grease a 2 quart casserole dish

4 cups thinly sliced spuds	2 tablespoons butter
1/2 cup chopped onion	1/2 cup catsup
1 tablespoon flour	1 tsp Worcestershire
1 1/2 tsp salt	3 drops hot sauce
1/3 tsp pepper	1 cup shredded cheese
1 1/2 cups scalded milk	

4 strips bacon diced, cooked crisp and drained for topping.

Combine flour, salt and pepper. Layer the spuds, onion, flour mix and cheese in the casserole. Combine the liquids and pour over the spuds. Dot with butter, cover and bake for 45 minutes. Uncover, stir, bake another 15 minutes. Spuds should be tender. Sprinkle on cheese and top with bacon. 4-6 servings.

Creamed Onions

4 medium sweet onions peeled and quartered
a couple pinches of salt and pepper

1/2 cup fat free half & half
1 tsp flour

Cook the onions over medium heat with just enough water to steam tender. Salt and pepper lightly. Blend the half & half and flour until smooth and pour over the onions and cook until sauce thickens. Pour into a bowl and sprinkle with herb flavored croutons that have been crushed. You can also microwave.

Mixed Veggies on the cold side

3 cups of mixed vegetables frozen or fresh
1 medium sweet onion
Optional: 3 tablespoons raisins and salted cashews
Use your choice from the Dressings section.

Steam the vegetables crisp tender and cool. Slice the onion in very thin slices and separate the rings. Add your choice of dressing and toss gently. Add raisins and cashews. Serve with sandwiches or sliced cold meat.

Scalloped Potatoes skinny style

Preheat to 350 degrees
Grease 2 quart casserole dish

4 cups spuds sliced thin	1/4 tsp pepper
1-2 tsp butter substitute	1 tsp dried onion
2 tablespoons flour	1 1/2 cups can skim milk

Place sliced spuds in bowl and add the melted butter and toss to coat. Combine the flour, pepper and onion. Layer the spuds in a 2-3 quart casserole. Alternate with the flour mix. Pour the skim milk over the top. Bake for 60-70 minutes uncovered. Sprinkle some low fat cheese, chopped sausage or ham on top.

MICROWAVE - covered 15-18 min, stir every 4-5 minutes.

SALADS

Sauerkraut Slaw

2 cans or 2 1/2 cups kraut washed and drained well

1/2 cup oil	1/2 cup onion chopped fine
1 cup sugar	1/4 cup green pepper chopped
1/2 cup vinegar	1/2 cup celery chopped
1/2 tsp salt	12 stuffed green olives, sliced

Make a dressing of the oil, sugar, salt and vinegar. Pour over the kraut and mix well. Add onion, green pepper, celery and the olives. Let stand several hours to season. Drain slightly before serving as mixture can be juicy.

Crazy Noodle Salad

1/4 cup rice vinegar	1/4 cup thin sliced onions
2 tablespoons sugar	1/4 cup raisins
4 tablespoons soy sauce	1/3 cup sliced almonds

1 tablespoon sesame oil or canola
1 pkg ramen oriental noodles broken up in pieces
Nice selection of lettuce greens and cut vegetables

Mix the first four ingredients together. In a big salad bowl place your selections of greens and vegetables.

Add the onions, almonds, raisins and noodles. Pour the dressing over the salad and toss.

Chicken Salad

2 cups diced cooked chicken   1/2 cup celery
1/3 cup french dressing   1/2 cup pineapple bits
1/2 cup mayonnaise   1/2 cup seedless grapes
1/4 cup toasted almond slivers

Marinate cooked chicken overnight in the french dressing. At serving time, mix chicken and all the other ingredients together with the mayonnaise.

MAIN DISHES

Plain Ol' Beans and Ham

1 lb great northern beans
1 large ham bone with meat <u>OR</u>
4-6 meaty ham hocks
1-2 cups jellied ham broth <u>OR</u>
1 large can chicken broth

Garnishes:
1 onion chopped fine <u>or</u> green onion tops chopped fine
Herb or bacon flavored croutons

In a stainless steel kettle, add 3 quarts of water and the beans. Bring to a boil, cover and cook on medium heat for one hour. Let stand 30 minutes then drain and add ham bone or hocks, broth, onion and enough water to just cover the beans. Place back on medium heat and cover. Cook until beans are tender. Serve in bowls with a sprinkle of onions and/or croutons on top and fresh ground pepper. 4-6 generous servings.

Hints: You can use beef ribs. Sear the meat and add to the beans with beef stock. A touch of garlic ramps it up a bit. Add cooked chopped carrots, celery, parsnips or diced potatoes during last 10-15 minutes of cooking. The vegetables should be just heated through, not mushy.

...{{ Home for Lovin' }}...

All of us here at Martha's agree that we couldn't let the day go by without mentioning the best ribs we've ever eaten. And she's been pretty quiet up until now, so Martha should have to tell the story.

"There's one family in a neighboring town that everyone knows. George and Ruthie are special folks. They've raised 12 children - a 'yours, mine and ours family.' They just recently sold their print shop and are settling in to enjoy the grandkids and greatgrands.

"Over the years, many have passed their way in need of a place to stay, a job, recovering from illness, always something. They've taken them all in, healed their wounds and sent them out again into the world. Word spread over the years, kind of a network of sorts, and it wasn't unusual for them to get a call from their 'extended family' about someone in need - could they help, did they have room?

"When my mother and Bud both had multiple surgeries a month apart, I spent the better part of six months at their house. I slept on a cot between my two patients' rooms. The Shrivers, bless their hearts, they never asked for anything. George said our friendship was all they needed.

"Their big house was always in need of cleaning and I did what I could when the patients were resting or sleeping. Since Ruthie and George worked long hours at the shop, I made sure they had a hot evening meal. Then, there was always a game or two of cards after supper. George loved to play cards and even as tired as he was after a full day, he could remember every card that had been played including what you had remaining in your hand. He loved to win and looking back, that may be why he kept score.

"Into this mix, the grown kids would pop in with their families and there would be a houseful. Pandemonium would reign supreme for a couple of hours, and then everyone would go home to put the kids to bed, or if it was the weekend, everyone camped out on the floor. Ruthie said she could never stand a quiet house after the children were gone, so we would have another game of cards, or we would visit while I rubbed their feet and backs until sleep filled their eyes.

"My heart is full when I think of how they opened up their home to me, a stranger to them, and loved me as one of their own. All of us at the table here who have known them admit we still go back to their house for a quick fix."

And here is the country rib recipe she always cooks when 'the family comes home for lovin'. Ruthie couldn't give exact amounts because she cooks a whopping amount at a time, but she said this would do the trick for a family of four.

Country Spare Ribs

<u>Place in a stainless steel kettle the following</u>:
Spare ribs with bone (enough for your family)
Couple of onions quartered
1 tsp peppercorns
2 tsp salt

Cover ribs with water and bring to a boil. Turn to medium-high heat, cook for 30 minutes uncovered. Remove the kettle from the stove and take out the ribs. Save the rib water to use for soups, stews or flavoring beans. Place the ribs in a roasting pan (I use my turkey roaster) and throw in some chopped garlic on the top and cover with a couple of bottles of barbecue sauce or your own sauce. Those ribs should be covered in sauce. Cover and bake in a 350 degree oven at least one hour or until done.

Hot Puppies

2 beaten eggs
1 cup canned milk
1/2 tsp salt
2 pkg of good meat wieners

2 cups flour
2 tsp baking powder
1/4 tsp soda

While heating the deep fat fryer, insert wooden skewers at least 1 1/2 inches into the wieners. You can do this ahead of time and refrigerate until time to cook them. Mix the batter in a deep bowl. Dip each wiener in the batter and then fry until golden brown. Serve hot with a sweet smoked mustard and catsup.

...{{ First Turkey }}...

Well, Marsha's going to be late today but she called in her recipe last night by phone. And I gotta tell you girls I never laughed so hard in my life when she told me this story.

She and Cory were newly married and her in-laws were coming for Thanksgiving. There was only one problem, Marsha was new to ranch cooking. She knew her soon-to-be company would be checking everything out. You know, seeing if she passed muster. She opened up her New Bride's cookbook and flipped the pages to ROAST TURKEY AND STUFFING. Rolling up her sleeves, she surveyed the kitchen determined to make a GRADE A mouthwatering turkey with all the trimmings. Like any cooking novice, she faithfully followed the instructions in her cookbook.

Preheat your oven to 350 degrees. Okay, next was the bird and stuffing. She had done all the prep work the night before so now this would be the easy part. Everything was going nicely. She had the spuds scrubbed and ready to boil for mashers. Salads and dessert were in the walk-in cooler. Rereading the steps in her book, it looked like a easy lope to the finish line. She breathed in and heaved the "I'm in control" sigh. You know the one, girls, we've all been there.

She had just placed the stuffed turkey in the roaster when the in-laws arrived - early, wouldn't you know it? Quickly placing the roaster in the oven, she checked everything out, nothing burning, table was set, flowers arranged and Cory, bless him, was pouring the drinks.

Betty, the mother-in-law, was a grand person. She knew Marsha was a city girl and trying very hard to fit in and find her place in ranch family life. Maybe too hard. Marsha was nervous and Betty's heart went out to her.

"Okay, now," Betty smiled, "hugs all around." Everyone laughed and greetings were exchanged. They all settled in for a visit before the football games started. The snacks and refreshments were polished off during the games.

Once in a while, Marsha went in to check on the turkey. She reviewed the cookbook ... yes sir, everything was just fine, but the turkey didn't look like it was cooking very well. Cory came into the kitchen and after a brief discussion, he went out and checked the fuse box and then the plug and cord in behind the stove. No, everything was fine. "Don't worry about it honey, just go relax." he said, putting one arm over her shoulders and walking her back into the living room.

An hour before the sit-down dinner, the women went into the kitchen to start the final preparations. Betty said she would peek at the turkey and opened the oven door to take the lid off the roaster. Marsha noticed her mother-in-law had the roaster lid half raised and asked her what was wrong.

"Well, I'm not sure," said Betty with a puzzled look. "I swear that bird isn't any darker in color than two hours ago. Cory checked out the stove didn't he?" She removed the lid and checked out the turkey again.

"Yes, Mom, he did." Marsha stepped over to the stove and looked at the bird. Her hands flew up to her face, covering her eyes. "Oh no! That turkey looks awful."

The poor bird was white as a ghost. You could see little white goosebumps where the feathers had been, and the turkey juice was oozing from every one of them. The turkey looked like it needed a vitamin shot. Then the new bride began to cry. Everything had been going so well.

"Now, dry those tears. Sometimes you have to be a detective in your own kitchen. We all have kitchen snafus that we have to figure out." Betty pulled out a hanky and dabbed her daughter-in-law's eyes. "Let's go back over everything from step one," she winked.

They started checking off every step in the cookbook. Yes, the oven had been preheated. Marsha looked at the dial, yes it was on preheat. Betty took a step over and looked at the dial on the stove, back at the cookbook and then at her daughter-in-law.

"Marsha, dear, your turkey has been taking a sauna instead a suntan," her mother-in-law said, smiling and shaking her head. "The dial is still on preheat."

"What!" screamed Marsha. "You mean that turkey is ... is ..." and then she started laughing, "a steamed up bird?" Betty joined in and pretty soon they were laughing so hard they were crying. "Ohhh," Marsha's teary eyes widened and she whispered, "I don't have another turkey."

Hamburgers, hot dogs, and spuds go down just fine on Thanksgiving. It's family that counts.

Chicken Fried oven-style

Preheat oven to 400 degrees
A big baking sheet to hold the chicken pieces

1 chicken cut up in pieces	1 tsp paprika
1 cup flour	1 tsp ground pepper fresh
1 tsp salt	1/2 cup butter or oil

Set cut up chicken aside and mix the rest together in a shallow bowl. In a no-stick baking sheet or pan, melt 1/2 cup butter or oil, just enough to layer the bottom of the pan. Roll each chicken piece in the flour mixture and place meat side down on the pan. Bake for 30 minutes, turn pieces over and bake another 30 minutes. Many of us use the frozen boneless chicken cuts now.

Ground Beef Supreme

1 lb of lean ground beef	1 tsp salt
3 tablespoons mince onion	1/4 cup chopped celery
1 egg beaten	1/2 cup water
1/4 cup bread crumbs	1 can cream soup
	(your choice)

Mix everything together but the soup and water. Shape into 1 inch thick patties - square or oval. Brown in a skillet with a little oil to prevent sticking. Carefully turn the meat over and brown the other side. Mix soup and water and pour over the meat and cook slowly for about 20-30 minutes. Remove the meat and add some fresh ground pepper to the gravy. Serve with mashed spuds and green beans. Leftovers are a great base in stew.

COOKIES

Gladys is sharing her gingersnaps with us today. On cold days, there is nothing like a ginger cookie and a cup of coffee. Not too long ago, she put these out on the kluckers' table and, diet or no diet, they were gone. Gladys needs to tell the story before she puts the recipe in the pile.

...{{ Buckaroo Snaps }}...

"Alda and Don Stensen were the best kind of folk. He'd cowboyed his way from Kansas to the west coast and was still buckarooing for the local ranchers. Alda had been a school teacher when one-room or sodhouse schools were in every little town, and she stayed active in the local church and helped out at the grade school.

"I was having coffee with them one day, when one of the local ranchers came by and asked Don if he could saddle up and ride. He needed an extra hand for a couple of days to bring his cattle down off the mountain before calving started. Grub for man and horse would be provided as usual. Don nodded and looked over at his wife as he went out to get Sugar ready for the trailer ride up the mountain. Alda went to the freezer to grab a pack of gingersnaps - her husband's favorite. A ready supply was always available in her big chest freezer.

"A few days later, Alda called and asked if I could run some "snaps" and sandwiches out to Don. Her old banger of a car wouldn't start. Don and the others driving the herd down the mountain had been having nothing but problems the whole trip. Now, they were about 15 miles up the road and things hadn't improved any. She didn't know if he'd make it back in time for supper. I agreed since I was on my way to town anyway.

"About 12 miles up the road, I saw them trailed out along the highway for quite a stretch. Two out-of-state cars went through ahead of me, laying on their horns and scattering cattle every direction. There was a lot of traffic on the country highway that day, and these idiots didn't realize honking and ramming their way through the mass of hide and hooves could be dangerous business.

"By the time the herd was back on track, the dogs and men looked worn out. Off in the ditch, I spotted Don leaning forward in the saddle, hollering at two old stubborn bossies the dogs were bringing up the bank. I rolled down the window and yelled out that I had his buffet dinner in a sack. He waved and turned Sugar towards the car. They pushed through five or six more cows to get to the driver's door.

"Well, now, aren't you a pretty sight? I said. He was bundled up against the cold, but his eyes were pretty bleary and his craggy face was chapped a bit from the cold air even with a couple of days head start on a beard. Cinder-fine dirt covered his hat and coat. He removed his kerchief from around his nose and mouth, slapping it against his thigh to remove the fine dust.

"It's been one heckuva ride, he said raspily.

"I bet you know each one of those beasts personally by now, I smiled.

33

"He looked down the highway towards the trailing cattle and narrowed his eyes against the cold sun. There was no warmth in his smile. *I don't know about the personal part,* Don said, *but I sure as hell got a name for every one of 'em.*"

Gingersnaps

Preheat oven to 350 degrees
Grease a cookie sheet

4 cups flour	2 tsp ginger
4 tsp baking soda	1 1/2 cups shortening
1 1/2 tsp salt	2 cups sugar
2 tsp cinnamon	1/2 cup molasses
2 tsp cloves	2 eggs

Sift dry ingredients together and set aside. Cream shortening and sugar together. Slowly add the molasses. Beat in one egg at a time. Add the dry ingredients. Form into teaspoon size balls. Place on the cookie sheet and bake until light brown. Makes a whole bunch and freezes well.

Biscuit Cookies

Preheat oven to 400 degrees
Grease cookie sheet or use cooking spray

3 1/4 cups flour	1 egg
1 tsp soda	1 1/2 tsp vanilla
1/2 tsp salt	1 tsp nutmeg
1/2 cup soft margarine	1/2 cup sour cream
1 cup sugar	

*Substitute cottage cheese for sour cream by blending cheese to cream consistency to equal 1/2 cup.

Sift flour, soda, salt. Use a kitchen counter type mixer, not a hand held mixer and use the flat beater. Cream the margarine and sugar. Add the egg and flavorings. Beat 2 minutes. With your mixer on low speed, alternate adding part of the sour cream and flour to the egg mixture to form a dough. The dough should be soft and pliable like biscuit dough. You can add a tad more flour, but watch out. If dough is stiff, you've too much flour - see below for saving face and it won't be cookies!

Turn out on floured board and roll out to desired thickness - 1/2 to 3/4 inch. Cut with biscuit or cookie cutter and place on baking sheet. Bake 8-10 minutes. Cookies will finish cooking while cooling. You want them tender like biscuits. Cool on a rack. The cookies carry well in coffee cans to picnics, baseball games, fishing and hunting trips. You can glaze them.

Outguessed the recipe and have a stiff dough? Heat up your deep fryer and pinch off good sized chunks of the dough and deep fry. Drain and roll in cinnamon sugar or powdered sugar. Serve immediately.

···{{ Auntie Eunice }}···

Alice has one of the best cookie recipes for company, holidays, really just about anytime. She gets pretty emotional when she talks about this gal, but it's a great story. Go Alice, we've got the tissues ready.

"Aunt Eunice was the number one cookie maker around. She was not really my aunt, but she was 'auntie' to the neighborhood and really special. A small, squarely built woman with short curly ash brown hair streaked with grey, she was Mrs. Santa Claus to many kids. Wire-rimmed pincer glasses sat atop her nose for reading recipes, and there was always a pretty apron covering her navy blue house dress.

"She and Bob had retired from the ranch and lived next door to us when we were townies. Our houses were about five feet apart separated only by a chicken wire fence. Her kitchen door faced our house and the fence. I was young and too scared to go in through her front door on the street side because there was a bobcat skin mounted on the wall by the door. She had shot the cat while it was raiding the hen house one ranch winter. Those glassy green eyes stared right at me and ... it had teeth ... I could almost hear it growl. But, I was not to be denied her cookies, and I had placed two old rickety chairs on either side of the fence between the houses. When you are only 5, you need a boost to get up and over.

"Her kitchen was a heaven of many delightful smells - sugar, spice, flour, coffee brewing, roast in the oven and goodies baking. The red and grey speckled lineolum was spotless. White tiled counters were covered with various baking utensils and shiny stainless steel equipment in one stage or other of measuring or mixing.

"Bob had built her a breakfast nook by the kitchen door with comfortable stools for sitting and visiting.

She had embroidered and crocheted the multi-colored seat pads. As I remember, she always had a basket of knitting or crocheting in every corner of the house. Her hands were never still, always creating, always doing something.

"I spent a lot of time in her kitchen, sampling cookies and other treats, drinking milk and talking. If I was crying, hurt or felt bad, I would find myself on her kitchen step calling out "Auntie Eunie, I want a cookie." I can still hear the soft clipped voice soothing away my doubts and fears. She was a great listener and kids need that even today. She needed it, too. She said the kids kept her young at heart with a zip in her step. Here's the one all the kids loved best, and I know Auntie Eunie would be pleased."

Someone hand Alice a tissue. In fact, make it a whole box.

Aunt Eunice's Bird Nests

Preheat oven to 350 degrees

1/2 cup butter	1/4 cup brown sugar
1 cup flour	1 egg white whisked foamy
1 egg yolk	Jelly

2/3 cup fine chopped or ground nuts (walnuts or pecans work best, but experiment)

Mix butter, sugar, flour and yolk together. Form into 1/2 inch balls. Roll the balls in the whisked egg white and then in the nuts. Place on a cookie sheet and press down with the bottom of glass. Bake 5 or 6 minutes. Pull out and dent the center of each cookie with the back of a spoon. Place a bit of jelly in the dented center and return to the oven for 5 more minutes - no longer! They may look underdone, but they are not. Set on racks to cool. Makes 30 cookies.

DESSERTS - BREADS

It turns out there are two good recipes on the table today and they both have very good stories. So we'll just tell 'em both.

...{{ Beloved Mary }}...

Most of us can trace our roots back to other older countries in the world. Aunt Ida's older cousin Mary was a recent immigrant when Ida was young. Aunt Mary, as she was known to everyone around, had come from the Austrian area as a young girl. She spoke several languages and landed herself a job working at the nation's capitol as an interpreter. Life was good and full of new experiences.

A young businessman and widower started courting her. He had a grand home in the Midwest, a thriving business and a small son to raise. They married before leaving New York and made the arduous journey west by train and wagon. She soon discovered that her husband had not been entirely truthful with her. Her new home was a sod house next to his trading post on an Indian reservation. His son was barely a year old.

What a blow that must have been. She set about trying to make the best of it. She became friends with

Ida's mother, Rose, who was also from an Austrian immigrant family and lived a few miles down the road. They could speak English, yes, but they were more comfortable talking in languages they were both familiar with.

Allen liked to "drink with the men" and the trading post lost business. It wasn't long before Mary had decided she couldn't take it and went to stay with Rose until the train came. In those days, a woman who left her husband or divorced him was not considered much better than a prostitute. Being a widow was okay, but it was a black mark against a "good woman" that left her husband even if he was basically lazy and made no attempt to really support his family. Society in those days wasn't very tolerant, and Rose was afraid the young woman would be shunned. It would ruin her life. She managed to talk the young bride out of leaving. Mary had a hard life, and Rose often regretted she had advised her friend to stay.

Mary's cooking skills became known throughout the area, and she opened a small cafe in the trading post. Her kolachi and cream pies brought in folks from all over. The cafe kept body and soul together when Allen was in a drinking and bragging mood, having spent all the spare cash on a round or two at the tavern.

Well, it's about time Aunt Ida showed up. She's been around the corner of the kitchen sampling the goodies and listening. Get your coffee Ida and sit down here. You'll have to finish the story about Mary.

"As she got older, she got wider. Having lived a life full of hard work and little rest, the body parts were worn out. She walked with a cane and the small flowered print dresses clung tightly to her heavily bosomed frame. Black laced shoes with old fashioned cotton stockings hid broken down veins and feet. The hair on her head was thin and snow white now. There were lines and creases of disappointment, but the eyes twinkled with secrets and mischief. And being crippled up with arthritis certainly didn't stop her from loving life.

"Any family member Aunt Mary visited looked forward to seeing her and, of course, her kolachi. On the last snowy visit to see my mother, they made kolachi together. Singing and talking in several languages, they laughed their way through two or three batches. There were samples to be tasted at the large, wooden, clawfooted kitchen table and then washed down with steaming cups of hot cocoa. It was something we all remembered, because it was the last time these two would be together on this Earth. Not long after the visit, Mary was gone through this vale of tears, and it was a hard time for all of us.

"There was a huge gathering at our house after the services. Mother had gone out to the freezer to get some frozen dessert for the crowd of folks. When she didn't come back to the kitchen, I went to look for her. She was sitting on a stool by the open freezer, cradling in her hands a package of Mary's frozen kolachi from that last day together.

"Eyes brimming with tears, she sighed, *This is a very sad time ... I have lost my dearest friend.* Then, shaking her head and wiping her eyes with the back of her hand, she said, *But I would be dishonoring her memory if I did not serve her finest gift to us.* And so together, we brought the last treasure Aunt Mary left us to be shared in laughter and memories, as it was meant to be."

Eee gad, girls, you're all gonna run me out of nose wipes. Alice, you'd better give me a couple.

Aunt Mary's Kolachi

1 cup milk	2 1/2 to 3 cups flour
1/4 cup butter	3 egg yolks
1/2 cup sugar	1 pkg yeast in 1/2 cup
1 tsp salt	warm water

Scald the milk and add butter, sugar and salt. Cool to warm. Add the yeast and 1 1/2 cups of the flour. Beat 5 minutes. Add the eggs and beat again. Add enough flour to make the dough barely firm enough to handle. Turn out onto a floured board and knead immediately. Cover dough and raise in a warm place. Roll out and cut into squares (or rounds) and place on a greased cookie sheet. Add 2 teaspoons of filling to the center. Pinch the corners together in the center holding the filling inside. Put a pinch of topping on each kolachi. Cover and raise. Bake at 400 degrees for 12 to 20 minutes depending on the size of your kolachi.

Prune Filling: Cook and pit dried prunes, remove all juice possible and chop fine.

Cottage Cheese Filling: To 2 cups dry cottage cheese, add 1 egg, 2 tablespoons sugar, and a dash of nutmeg.

<u>Topping</u>:
3 tablespoons flour
2 tablespoons sugar
1/3 quarter butter or margarine

Combine the topping. It should be crumbly. With a spoon or your fingers put a large pinch on each and pat lightly to hold in place.

...{{ Tea with Grosse }}...

Several of the old gals here love a sweet bread and Martha has always baked a loaf for the snaggletoothed crowd. We've asked her to put that recipe on the table today, with the story of course.

"I loved it when my mother and I went to tea at Grosse's house. We would dress up in our best and take a small gift - a jar of jelly, fresh cut flowers, a box of treats, or a book. Reaching up I rang the doorbell and waited for the tap, tap, tap of her heels on the polished hardwood floor as she came to the door. It opened into a world of a different age.

"She was from the 'old country.' Manners and civility were an important part of her life. She had weathered all the things humans do, including economic hard times that left her and her husband without funds. It was hard for the family to go from being very well-to-do to poor. But they made it through and although she wasn't rich, she was comfortable in her old age.

"Persian rugs dotted the floors, a grandfather clock filled the corner by the kitchen, richly wooded china cupboards with etched glass held her family's treasures, and the windows were framed by real lace drapes caught up on each side with white satin tassels.

"Light filtered through the sitting room across an overstuffed, ornately wood-carved sofa, comfy chairs and the most beautiful coffee table I have ever seen. The intricately carved top showed a hunting scene and was protected by a piece of glass etched along the sides to give the illusion of snow falling.

"Lovely matching china cups and saucers, sugar, creamer, and dessert plates were set out on the crocheted linen cloth covering the center of the table. Fine linen napkins pillowed the silverware at each place setting. Wonderful aromas drifted in from her tiny kitchen, and I could hear the teakettle singing. A rattling of the teapot lid signaled her entrance with the tray of hot tea and lemon glazed bread.

"Grosse set the tray on the table and motioned with her right hand for us to be seated. The grand tea opera began. Unfolding her napkin, she laid it in her lap in one fluid motion and waited for us to do the same. The tea was then poured with her doing the honors for the first serving of '*one lump or two?*' The bread was precisely cut and each piece slid skillfully onto a dessert plate and presented to us as though it were the grand prize. My mother had spent time in Europe and they visited, laughed and told stories about their travels and experiences. I concentrated on that wonderful lemon tea bread and more tea.

"When everyone was 'tead and breaded,' we made a tour of her small garden. Ideas and advice flowed quickly between the two avid gardeners, and sometimes there was a cutting or a small packet of seeds exchanged. Our stroll to the garden gate signaled the end of a lovely stay. I think about her on warm summer days, and wish I could be 'tead and breaded' in style one more time."

In fact, we are about to have some slices and tea right now. This recipe comes close to that lovely fragrant bread.

Lemon Tea Bread

Preheat oven to 350 degrees
Grease and flour a good sized loaf pan

1/2 cup milk	1 1/2 cups flour
1 cup sugar	1 tsp baking powder
2 eggs	1 tsp salt
1 1/2 tsp grated lemon peel	1/2 cup chopped pecans
1/3 cup melted butter or margarine	

Combine in a big bowl the milk, sugar, eggs, melted butter and lemon peel. Beat at medium speed until blended. Add the dry ingredients and mix at low speed until the batter is smooth and moist. Fold in the pecans. Pour into the greased loaf pan. Bake between 40-50 minutes until done.

Glaze:

While bread is baking combine 1/3 cup sugar and 4 tablespoons fresh lemon juice. Bottled juice gives the bread a slightly different flavor. Set aside.

When the bread is done, leave it in the pan and place on a wire rack to cool. Poke holes in the bread with a toothpick so the glaze can sink in. Slowly pour the glaze over the hot bread. Cool 10 minutes and remove the bread to finish cooling on the rack. Once it is completely cold, you can wrap it up and store in refrigerate or freezer. Depending on the size of slice you cut, it makes between 14 and 25 slices.

DESSERTS - CAKES AND FROSTINGS

Evelyn's Ivory Frosting

3 tablespoons flour	1 cup butter
1 cup milk	1 cup sugar
	1 tsp vanilla

Make a paste of the flour and milk and cook, stirring until it has a smooth custard consistency. Cool to COLD -- not lukewarm, but cold. Cream butter, sugar and vanilla. Combine with the COLD custard. Spread on your cake.

...{{ Lover's Cake }}...

Aunt Ida brings us this story about Rose and her chocolate cake. She brought the cake! Look at those slices of cake, girls!

"During the Depression, college students boarded with families around the town. There wasn't a lot of money and everyone did what they could to keep food on the table. The football team boarded upstairs in my mother's house which was just a good stretch of the legs from the college campus.

"She was known for her cooking and midwifery skills throughout the local area. It wasn't unusual for the 'boys' to bring a couple of extra chums home for supper. There weren't any fancy tiny food groups delicately placed on colorful china to sooth the artful stomach. Stick-to-your-ribs food and plenty of it, was her stock in trade.

"In the spring the young men turned from the aggressive pursuit of a pigskin ball to setting their sights on easier game - or so they thought. There was a beautiful small orchard between her house and the campus. It was here that the boys developed a new course of study.

"It was called Orchard. You could get any number of hours of Orchard, but that depended on the girl you were courting or sparking. One player in particular, Jess, would tell Mom, *Well, Ma, you won't have to set a place for me tonight. I've got a full course meal coming with a couple of hours of Orchard.* That meant fried chicken, potato salad and lemonade or iced tea plus the attention of a lovely young woman. Jess had to bring the chocolate cake, and Mom always gave in and made the cake.

"The orchard continued to be a pretty popular spot and soon my mother's cake became known as the Lovers' Cake. It was quick and simple. Before long, the cake was used by women throughout the valley.

"Woe be unto the unsuspecting hunter who is really the hunted and baited by chocolate!"

Lovers' Cake

Preheat oven to 350 degrees
Grease and flour cake pans or a 9x12 pan

3 cups flour
1 tsp baking soda
1 tsp salt
6 tablespoons cocoa
2 cups sugar

2 cups water
3/4 cup oil
2 tablespons vinegar
2 tsp vanilla

Sift all the dry ingredients. Add the liquids. Stir together. DO NOT BEAT. Pour into greased and floured pan or pans. Bake 25-30 minutes.

Auntie Eunice's Applesauce Cake

Preheat oven to 350 degrees
Grease a 9x12 pan

1 1/2 cups flour
1 tsp baking soda
1 tsp cinnamon
1/2 tsp cloves
1/2 tsp nutmeg

1 cup sugar
1/2 cup shortening
1 cup applesauce
1 tsp vinegar
1 cup raisins or dates

*1/4 cup nuts chopped (optional)

Sift the flour and spices. In a mixing bowl, cream the sugar and shortening, then add the vinegar and applesauce. Dissolve the soda in a little hot water, let it foam and stir into the applesauce. Add the spiced flour and stir well. DO NOT BEAT. Fold in the raisins and the nuts. Pour into the pan and bake 45 minutes. Cool on a rack.

DESSERTS - PIES

...{{ You're in the Army Now, Bride }}...

Martha's mother was a real world traveler, courtesy of the US Army. She's shared with us often the family photos and keepsakes from that time. And, after all that bragging about her mom's banana cream pie recipe, she's handing it over today.

"My mother followed my dad through his years with the Army. She made one journey as a new young wife to Europe right after WW2 in 1946 on a reconditioned troop ship with other wives and families.

"Europe was still war-torn. There were burned out buildings, no sewer systems or fresh water in some areas, and displaced persons, or 'DPs' as they were called, from other countries flooding into the Allied held areas. Some supplies were hard to come by, and the women who decided to brave the after-war frontier to be with their soldier husbands made do with what they could get.

"The Russian line was not far from where mother and the other service families were housed in town, and the women chose to stay together in one apartment when their men had to be gone on maneuvers. Here they exchanged letters and photographs from home, traded recipes and sewing patterns, played pinochle and bridge, darned clothes and pressed the men's uniforms, even their underwear! That's right, there was no dry cleaners around the corner.

"When possible, they threw their resources together for a brunch. Most of these women had never been in conditions like this before, and the brunch days kept their sanity. If the military store, the 'PX,' didn't have the supplies needed, they would barter with local folks who were desperate for sugar, coffee, flour and tobacco. These seem such minor commodities to us here today in the land of plenty, but those people had practically nothing left -- no crops, no money, no family, sometimes no home or just a burned out shell for a home. Where there's a will, there's a way with a little bartering thrown in.

"This banana cream pie recipe is the one my mother made over after a foraging expedition for one of those brunches."

Ann's Banana Cream Pie

3/4 cup canned milk	3 yolks whisked
3/4 cup water	3 tablespoons butter
1/2 cup sugar	1/2 tsp vanilla
1/8 tsp salt	4 bananas sliced

6 tablespoons flour
1/2 pint whipping cream whipped to stiff peaks
1 pie crust baked in pie tin - 9 inch

Scald the milk. Mix the sugar, salt, flour and the water in a 2 quart saucepan. Stir in the scalded milk, cook about 5 minutes until thickened, stirring constantly. Add egg yolks slowly and cook for 1 minute. Add butter and vanilla. Set the pudding aside to cool. You can cool the pudding faster by setting it in a kettle of ice cold water and stirring to remove the heat from the pudding. Once the pudding is cold, fold in the whipping cream.

Cut bananas in thin slices and cover the bottom and sides of the crust. Spoon 1/2 of the filling over the bananas and then add a second layer of sliced bananas. Spoon the rest of the filling into the pie shell and smooth the filling.

Since using raw egg whites is no longer safe, you can use a meringue mix or use whipped nondairy topping. Spread and swirl the topping on the pie and seal along the crust. Lightly broiler-brown the meringue for a few minutes. Refrigerate for 6 hours for pudding to set up.

Best Pie Ever

Preheat oven to 350 degrees
Grease a large pie tin

Pie part:

1 tablespoon sugar	1 tsp cinnamon
1/4 cup chopped walnuts	
4 cups thinly sliced apples, peeled and cored	

Topping:

1/2 cup margarine	1/3 cup honey
1 egg	1 cup flour
1/4 tsp salt	

Mix the pie part together and place in the prepared pie tin. Combine the topping and spread over the apples. Bake for 40 minutes. Cool on a rack. Serves 8-10.

DESSERTS - OTHER

...{{ Garden Cookin' }}...

These two stories and recipes come from Marge's side of the family. It sure hits home with a few of us.

"One of the things I miss today is my Grandpa Blake's garden. As a young man, he'd worked in a steel foundry. Unfortunately, in those days, they didn't have safety standards, and my Grandpa's lungs had suffered for it. He tired easily and couldn't get air in or out of his lungs. While he was recuperating, he would roam around the area taking cuttings of different kinds of plants and trees. Eventually he became a grower for one of the large nurseries in the area.

"Since he was around the house and garden much of the time, he would take youngsters out for a carrot, turnip, radish or whatever was available from nature's table. While we were munching, we were also learning about seeds, soil and how everything has its place and time for growing and harvesting. Ahh, he was a sly teacher.

"I had two favorite garden things besides being a free roaming garden rabbit - mudpies and raspberries. Grandpa had a shed right by the garden for tools and an assortment of potting paraphenalia. He made me a little bench and a make-believe scrap wood oven by the door so I could mix and bake my mud pies. Oh those were glorious times, when I could be muddy and wet! I had an assortment of old utensils for scooping and mixing, as well as a variety of rocks, sand and colored sticks for decorating the pies.

"Grandpa Blake had been the cook's helper on several occasions. He would cut big stalks of leafy rhubarb and help 'cool' my pies by fanning them with the big rhubarb leaves. However, when I selected some of his beautiful flowers for decoration, we had a difference of opinion. There was a real squawking when I started mixing vegetables into the mud pies. But negotiations started when I shimmied up one of the apple trees after a couple of prime candidates for a mud apple pie. My mother said Grandpa was just about scared out of what few years he had left on this side of Heaven when he saw me twelve feet up the tree on a tiny twig balancing on one foot to reach just the right apple.

"Mother, bless her, acted as the middleman, and Grandpa and I came to some terms. Anything low growing was mine, anything taller than I could reach, was his but he would share. He would pick the flowers so the plant wasn't destroyed. (I had a tendency to pull up the whole thing.) Together, we agreed to a small piece of the garden space for mud pie vegetables and designated a small section of the blackberries and raspberries, too. And, for every three mud pies I made, I had to give him one. We sealed our deal with some rhubarb bars and cold milk.

"These are treasured memories found now only in faded yellow photographs and a few old battered pie tins I have kept over the years. But I will share with you girls today my Grandpa's famous rhubarb bars."

Rhubarb Dreamy Bars

Preheat oven to 350 degrees

2 cups flour	10 tablespoons sugar
1 cup butter	

Combine and pat into a 9x13 pan. Bake for 15 minutes or until the edges are just browning. Place on cooling rack and add the filling.

Filling:

4 eggs	3/4 tsp salt
2 cups sugar	4 cups diced rhubarb
1/2 cup flour	

Beat the eggs until creamy. Add sugar and beat. Stir in flour and salt. Fold in the rhubarb. Pour over the crust. Bake 45 minutes. Cool on rack. Serve with sour cream, whipped topping or ice cream.

...{{ Doggone Raspberries }}...

"Raspberries are still my favorite today. The bigger the berry, the better. I like the ones that are really big so you can get one on each finger and then eat them off your fingers one at a time. Joe just shakes his head, but doesn't say anything because he's just as daffy over cherries.

"Grandpa had a huge patch of raspberries, and they were always the best in the county. He said he sold only top berries because he had a granddaughter that cleaned up all the really ripe ones underneath. That was me alright. There are advantages when you are a child, and I could get under the raspberry bushes and glean out the fattest, ripest berries. There is no competition.

"In the summer, my parents never worried about me playing out front in the road with the rest of kids. I was out back under the cane stuffing my mouth with those sweet juicy berries. And I had help. Snipper was a black and white Boston bull terrier my dad brought home for me. He loved raspberries just as much as I did. So when he'd worked all the berries off the branches that he could reach, he'd come over to me and we'd share. I'd eat one and then feed one to him. Then I'd eat two and feed one to him. He didn't seem to care how many I ate, as long as he sampled some along the way.

"If anyone looked at Snipper and asked him if we were going to the raspberry patch, he would get up and make his way to the back door, sit down and stare back at us with such a look of longing in those deep dark eyes that it would send everyone into stitches of laughter. Humans are not the only ones with cravings that can't be satisfied."

Wild Bush Pudding

Preheat oven to 350 degrees
Grease medium casserole dish

1/2 cup sugar	1 tsp salt
1 egg	2 tsp baking powder
1/4 cup shortening	1/2 cup milk
1 cup flour	

2 cups strained blackberries or other caneberries

3/4 cup sugar
1 cup boiling water or fruit juice

Cream sugar, egg and shortening. Sift flour, baking powder, salt together. Add flour and milk to egg mixture and pour into the bottom of a casserole dish. Add on top in the following order: the berries, sugar and water or juice. Bake until dough comes up to the top. You can use a round cake or 8 inch square pan. Double the recipe for a 9x13 pan.

HOLIDAY TIME

Aplets

4 pkgs gelatin unflavored
2 1/2 cups applesauce
4 cups sugar

1 3-oz. pkg orange gelatin
1-2 tsp orange flavoring
2 cups nuts chopped fine

Combine for the coating:
1/2 cup powdered sugar

1/2 cup cornstarch

Before you start, grease a cookie sheet. Soak the unflavored gelatin in 1 cup of the applesauce for five minutes. Add everything but the nuts and flavor in a pan. Boil 15 minutes. Cool slightly. Add the nuts and flavoring. Pour onto the greased cookie sheet and chill 24 hours. Cut in squares and roll in the coating mix. Place candy on wax paper to set up for a couple of hours. Use wax paper between layers. Makes 2 lbs. Pack in tins or Christmas paper-wrapped boxes for delivery.

...{{ Holiday Surprises }}...

We've been talking about the holiday boxes of goodies that folks would leave for the mailman, paperboy and other people who provided services during the year. Part of our job as kids growing up together was to find containers for the treats during the year, and then in early December we would all pitch in and cover them in brightly colored paper and ribbon. We were pretty competitive and the containers were just about anything we could decorate.

The mailman was always a favorite, because you could peek out the window and watch him pull the brightly colored, packaged goodies out of the mailbox. Glancing around to see if anyone was looking, he reached into the decorated box and pulled out a piece of fudge. There was a smile and small sigh of satisfaction as the fudge was duly savored. Sometimes, he'd pop in a second piece, close his eyes and rock back and forth just a little bit on his heels and toes. Life can be sweetly filling and simple at times.

Rose's No Beat Fudge

Butter a large 9x12 pan

In a large bowl that will hold heat (like your mixer's stainless steel bowl) add:

2 16-oz. packages chocolate chips
3 squares baking chocolate cut up
1 cup walnut meats chopped (if you want nuts)
1 pint jar marshmallow cream
1 tsp vanilla

In a quart saucepan, bring to a boil:
4 1/4 cups sugar
1 can evaporated milk (not condensed)

Stir until sugar is dissolved and bring the mixture to a rolling boil. Continue stirring to keep from scorching and let it boil EXACTLY for 5 minutes. Pour the hot mixture over the bowl ingredients and stir and fold until the chocolates are completely blended. You can use your kitchen counter mixer and the paddle beater on low speed to fold and blend. Pour into the prepared pan and cool. Cut into squares before it cools completely. Unbelievable good stuff! Makes 2 lbs.

Aunt Mary's Penuche

This is brown sugar butter candy from the old country.
Make it exactly as directed - no substitutions.
Butter a 9x9 pan before you start.

1/4 pound butter
1/4 tsp salt
4 1/2 cups packed light brown sugar
1 cup evaporated milk (fresh milk will curdle)
1 teaspoon vanilla
2 cups chopped nuts (or no nuts)

Combine first four ingredients, stir and cook over medium high heat until the sugar dissolves. Continue stirring and when it reaches a rolling boil, cook to soft ball stage (about 10 minutes). Don't let it scorch! Remove from heat and cool to lukewarm. Add the vanilla and nuts. Beat until the candy loses its gloss. Immediately pour into the greased pan. Cut as soon as it cools, otherwise when it hardens you will have to break it apart. Makes 2 lbs.

Christmas Cookies

Preheat oven to 350 degrees
Grease cookie sheets
Large stainless steel cooking pot or bowl

5 cups flour	2 cups butter
2 tsp baking soda	4 eggs
2 tsp salt	2-3 tsp vanilla
2 tsp cinnamon	1/2 cup cream **or**
3 cups brown sugar	half & half

Chop or cut the following then set aside:

1 lb brazil nuts	2 lbs dates
1-2 lb walnuts	1 lb raisins
1 lb pecans	1/2 lb split blanch almonds
3 rings candied pineapple	16 oz box candied cherries

Take out 1/2 cup flour from the 5 cups and sprinkle on the fruit and nuts, mix to prevent sticking. Set the mixture aside. Sift remaining dry ingredients together. Cream butter and gradually add the sugar so the mixture is light and creamy. Add one egg at a time unbeaten and mix well after each. Add vanilla. Mix in the dry ingredients and cream slowly - alternating wet and dry. Turn the cookie mix out into a large stainless steel kettle or mixing bowl. Add the floured fruit and nuts.

Now comes the fun part. You get to mix it altogether with your hands. First, wash your hands thoroughly and dry with a clean dish towel not used for anything else. Mix until all the fruit, nuts and dough are stuck together. Now wash your hands again and dry them.

Drop by teaspoonful on greased baking sheets and bake for 10-13 minutes. Cool on grates and then pack in cans lined with wax paper to prevent cookies from sticking together. Let them age 2-4 weeks.

I prefer to use the full dough recipe but decrease or delete altogether the candied fruit and use only nuts, raisins, dates and figs. Recipe can be halved. It's a great one to fashion to your own family.

Caramel Corn

Preheat oven to 250 degrees
Roaster pan greased with cooking spray

4 cups of your choice of nuts, coconut, dried fruit, etc.
6 quarts of popped popcorn

1 cup butter	1 tsp vanilla
2 cups brown sugar	1/2 tsp baking soda
1 tsp salt	

1/2 cup light or dark corn syrup or honey

Place popped corn in the roaster pan. Mix the nuts or other goodies to be added after pouring the syrup over the corn.

Move the oven grate to mid or low level as you may need to change depending on your oven. Don't let it burn the bottom of the caramel corn.

Melt the butter in a deep saucepan and stir in the brown sugar, syrup and salt. Boil 5 minutes without stirring. Stir in soda and vanilla (it has a tendency to boil over, so pay attention). Gradually pour over the corn, add your goodies and mix well. Bake for one hour, stirring every 15 minutes. Cool, then break apart sections and store in a tightly covered big container or tin. Makes 5 quarts.

...{{ The Boot }}...

Alice, here, has a Christmas story that's going to finish up our recipe exchange day.

"Ollie Baker was a man my folks hired off and on to work out on the farm. He always was helping someone in need. Whether it was fixing a picket fence or a kind word of encouragement to a child while he fixed a busted trike, Ollie always seemed to be there.

"Just after harvest one year, our barn caught fire. Neighbors helped the folks get the horses out in time. Ollie knew my mama cat had moved her kittens to the barn loft and went in after them. Well he came flying out of the burning loft with the whole kaboodle, and broke his right leg.

"The break was a bad one. The cast couldn't come off for a couple of months, so Ollie didn't get out much. People began to realize just how much he'd been doing in his spare time. The kids came by to keep him company every day, but through the weeks of confinement, we'd decided that our friend needed to know how much everyone cared about him.

"A couple weeks before Christmas, the cast came off, and we were ready with our plan of action. When we were sure that Ollie had left the Doc's office, my brother and I sneaked in to talk to the sawbones, and he decided to join in the fun. There was a flurry of activity as all of us came together in the spirit of the season.

"Ollie came over for Christmas morning breakfast, and afterwards the family gathered in the living room. There in front of our tree was a brightly painted red cast pieced back together with tape, glue, twine and surgical stainless steel. Doc helped us sanitize and widen it a bit so everything would fit. We used some of the volunteer fire department's red paint for color. The finest medical cotton balls formed a big, white cuff on the boot top and around the toe hole. It was overflowing with cards and small gifts from folks in the community. 'Seems during the week before Christmas, word got around about what we were up to and everyone had made a contribution.

"In our area over the next few years, anyone laid up around the holidays was sure to '*get the boot.*' Being '*given the boot*' took on a whole new meaning."

The holiday goodies can be mailed to our servicemen and women everywhere who are protecting us and our freedoms. Now, I know that may not be politically correct today, but I am a daughter, wife, mother and niece of veterans of four wars. The other gals around the table are veteran-related, too, in some fashion. We should never forget them at any time but especially at the holidays. It's a hard time to be far away from those you love. Enclose a letter and let them know you care.

Oh, and call the Post Office in September to find out when you need to mail your packages and ask for packing instructions.

A few kitchen tricks we want to throw in, too.

- Use long handled tongs for hard-to-reach items in cupboards.
- Small scissors kept in a jar by the stove or counter can open freezer or plastic sacks and boxes.
- Cutlery trays in drawers hold packages of yeast, beaters, pastry brushes, biscuit/cookie cutters, etc.
- Post a shopping list inside the cupboard doors. Do the same in the laundry room.
- A plastic spatula handle can be used to remove air bubbles from full jars before sealing and canning.
- Automatic ice cube maker trays can hold jars of condiments or meat in your refrigerator.
- 8 oz yogurt cups make good freezer jam containers.
- Get a small plastic basket with lid for small items in the dishwasher.

Just pile the dishes, gals, I'll do them later. Well, we sure are glad you showed up. You've got a load of recipes to try out and come Christmas time, we'll be sure to include you in the goodie box wrapping. The men will come along, too. They say they're doing us a favor by taste testing all the goodies for vitamins and acting as the quality control experts. We girls think it's quantity control - they already know the quality.